CW01309505

THE CROWNED KING OF BOLLYWOOD AND RULER OF OUR HEARTS: SHAH RUKH KHAN

BY TANIA IOANNOU

Edited by Kathryn Long

First Edition Printing: October 2019

Published by KDP Amazon

Copyrighted TI 2019

INTRODUCTION

This is a poet's tribute to an extraordinary individual. He woke me up from the lethargy of pain and emptiness. He helped me find a spark of life after the tragic loss of my beloved daughter.

I hope to have captured, the heart, soul and thoughts of the admirers and followers of the superstar SHAH RUKH KHAN.

Thank you TedTalks Vancouver for introducing me to the moving, sensitive, inspiring world of SHAH RUKH KHAN.

Tania Ioannou

ACKNOWLEDGMENTS

My most sincere gratitude for the accomplishment of this work goes to the following wonderful people.

First and foremost, the muse of my inspiration:

SHAH RUKH KHAN: Indian actor, entertainer, producer, TV host and award functions. Active philanthropist, recipient of awards, accolades and 5 doctorate degrees. Founder of the Meer Foundation, devoted husband and father. Brother to many in the film fraternity, mentor and nurturer of new talent. Altruistic, compassionate, gentle, generous, humble, witty, powerful, loving human being. A global citizen who fits in any culture and society, acts as a role-model, inspiring millions to pursue their goals, follow their dreams, persist in hard work, respect women and children's rights and to be kind and generous.

For all the above, he has provided the motivation for me to pen all my sentiments of admiration, adoration, respect and wonder towards this phenomenal persona who is a precious gem, and blessed gift from heaven. He will forever remain a legend, a supernova on the global stage of humanity.

I cannot thank you enough dear Shah Rukh Khan Sir, for all the love and joy you have brought into our lives. God bless you and your lovely family.

MONIKA IOANNOU: My beloved daughter and best friend who shares my enthusiasm and love for Shah Rukh Khan. It was she who introduced me to SRK through the first film of his I saw, Fan, which we watched together. Since then, we haven't stop watching his movies and following his life. She supported and helped me in my artistic effort to write these poems. With her encouragement, guidance and help, by using her considerable computer skills, as well as spending precious time together, I was able to complete my task.

CHRIS ANDERSON: The head of the TED organization and Curator of TED Talks, for inviting Shah Rukh Khan to appear on TED Talks, Vancouver, Canada in 2017. Mr. Khan's brilliant talk titled, "Thoughts on Humanity, Fame and Love", became the motivation for me to seek information about this exceptional individual. SRK's talk opened my heart and helped me change my perception on life, after the devastating loss of my 23 year old daughter to a car accident. Chris' contribution to this project has made advice, assistance, innovation and constructive suggestions available to millions of people around the world.

    The only way I could hope to extend my gratitude for his unique project was to become a volunteer TED Talk translator from English to Greek, which I am happy and honored to do. In this way, I can put a small pebble on the path he has paved. Chris' willingness to help humanity, and the help I personally received through it, is greatly appreciated.

JULIET BLAKE: Head of Television for TED Talks, movie producer and the Curator of Special Projects at TED is responsible for the production of 'TED talks India Nayi Soch 2017," hosted by Shar Rukh Khan on Indian Television. A huge success in India, and other countries world, saw millions of people watching the show with the help of subtitles, many watching only for the love of Shah Rukh Khan. Heartfelt thanks to Juliet for her leadership and vision and lending her talents to a professional and well done production.

JITENDER RISHI PARMAR: My dear Indian, spiritual friend, author of the novel, "Once Lost, Found Forever," assistant professor and enlightened soul. His support, encouragement, substantial help and soulful intervention in sending my book to Shah Rukh Khan's residence in India has showed me beautiful souls do exist everywhere and one can connect with them and feel a special bond even if they never meet in person. May God bless him.

SOCIAL MEDIA: Twitter, Facebook, YouTube and others, for access to information they provide to the public on Shah Rukh Khan. Many of SRK's interviews, quotes, talks, fan clubs, found on these sites, created the foundation to form my image of SRK. I found his mind, soul and personality revealed through the use of social media and used them to bring forth words poured out of my heart. My hope is to express the feelings in millions of other hearts, sharing the same love and admiration for Shah Rukh Khan and everything he stands for and personifies. If I have captured the thoughts and feelings of his admirers, even in the smallest way, then I have succeeded in my task.

KATHRYN LONG: A blessed friend, editor, author of novels, poetry and short stories. My soul-friend on this journey, helping me to realize my dream and accomplish my task in writing and making this book of poems possible. As my book's editor, she is the one responsible for correcting, rewriting, planning and generally organizing this whole project. Without her selfless support, my goal would not have been achieved. Her own comparable love and respect toward the influential superstar Shah Rukh Khan kept her going, despite various personal setbacks during the process of preparing the book. I extend my deepest gratitude to her for all the time, love and effort she put into this project. She was my guardian angel sent from heaven. Thank you, dear Kathryn.

I thank God and all the heavenly angels for enlightening me in writing these poems and for all the good people who have contributed to them, directly or indirectly, and all who either inspired or helped me make this dream a reality.

God bless you all!

Tania

Dear Dr. Shah Rukh Khan,

Were I to have been able to touch your heart and enter into a fraction of your soul with my poems, or in some way understand your sentiments, or somehow express a fragment of what you feel, (because no one can ever understand or know the real Shah Rukh Khan, except God himself), then my heart would be content.

However, my truest and deepest wish would be to have the honor of meeting you and experience the joy of reading some of my poems to you, in person.

INSHALLAH!

Tania Ioannou

CROWNED KING AND RULER: SHAH RUKH KHAN

TABLE OF CONTENTS

                                                              Page

1) SHAH RUKH KHAN (Acrostic).......................1

2) If (Parody)..2

3) You are precious to us....................................4

4) The Most Famous of Them All.......................5

5) My Name is Kh-Kh-Khan................................7

6) You Are the Reason for Making Us Smile.....8

7) Are You For Real?..10

8) What is it That Makes Him so Dear?............12

9) Oh Captain, My Captain................................14

10) I Have a Limerence on You...........................16

11) I Wish..18

12) Star light, Star Bright....................................19

13) He's the One and Only SRK..........................20

14) Dear Zindagi...22

TABLE OF CONTENTS cont'd

                                                              Page

15) This One's For the Crystal Award......................23
16) Only For You..24
17) Is it Real or a Utopia?..26
18) ''Welcome Pain''...27
19) Euphoria..29
20) The Road to Stardom..30
21) I Will Have Left My Mark...................................31
22) To My Angels in the Sky.....................................33
23) 2nd of November..34
24) Women of Power..36
25) Ted in India..38
26) For I am Love...40
27) When I Meet You..41

Ithaca Poem by C.P. Cavafy..42
Author Information...43

Shah Rukh Khan (Acrostic)

Sophisticated, self-made superstar
Honored, helpful humanitarian
Attractive, ageless artist
Hardworking, handsome heartthrob

Romantic, revolutionary royalty
Unique, unparalleled, universal
Keen, kindhearted kismet
Humorous, hotshot host

Knockout, knightly King
Humble heavenly Hero
Ambitious, accomplished Angel
Nominated, natural Nobility.

"IF"

If hardship and sorrow cannot defeat you,
in times of pain when you are feeling blue.
If victory and fame cannot deceive you,
your childish heart will always remain true.

If you grant forgiveness, not feeling bitter,
although slandered, wait for the truth to shine.
beingworshiped, not smitten by the glitter,
yet act sophisticated and divine.

If what you do is full of love and passion,
and you convey emotions full of zest.
If you not only feel but show compassion
to fellow humans, by doing your best.

If you don't take life's blessings for granted,
But yet you know you have done it "your way",
With great work, making people feel enchanted
and more worthwhile, at the end of the day.

(IF cont'd)

If you are determined to soar in the sky,
by peddling love and selling the world dreams.
Also making a name that will never die,
while nothing can ever be as it seems.

If you confront gossip by using humor,
and with your loved ones never wear a mask.
When only your presence creates a rumor
thus, making success such an easy task.

If life's challenges have named you a fighter,
and your chivalry has won people's hearts.
Your charm and wit has made your smile look brighter
and has established you a star in arts.

If talent has given you that special "zing",
and not just in Bollywood, you're "THE MAN".
Although humble, you're respected as a KING.

Then my friend, you are surely "SHAH RUKH KHAN!"

YOU ARE PRECIOUS TO US

Like a sculptural work of art, fragile yet tough.
Like a dazzling diamond, shiny yet rough,
Like a stormy gale sweeping up everything in its path.
As a past memory, making us cry and laugh.

A loving father and worthy brother as well.
A loyal husband casting a sweet spell.
You're the dream of the perfect son in every mother's heart,
Who's not only handsome, but sensitive and smart,

Possessing a sense of humor and witty mind."
You're also generous, caring and kind.
Like a luminous, shooting star, flaunting its glowing trail,
If we follow your path, our hopes will never fail.

You're a delicate soul which can fall into parts,
in order to please and conquer our hearts.
Like the light of our eyes and the sun's shine we cannot spare.
You are precious to us, *so we plead you "Take care"*.

THE MOST FAMOUS OF THEM ALL

Tell me moon and tell me sun
on the paths that you both roam,
behind horizons you rise and fall.
Who is the most famous of them all?

It is whispered in the wind
by the rustle of the leaves.
In the East there shines a brilliant star,
majestic and divine Avatar.

Raindrops spread it to the leaves,
as they cool and gently fall.
Ascending from earth to sky above,
there's only one who attracts our love.

Drifting clouds around the world,
caught sight of a hopeful smile.
It sent out grace to the human race,
through the innocent charm of his face.

(MOST FAMOUS cont'd)

Birds twittered about this myth,
as they travel far and wide.
He who fulfilled his ambitious dream,
is a global icon of esteem.

Ocean waves lapping the shore,
washed up this buzzword of truth.
He's a gifted artist, always first.
The pure water which quenches our thirst.

When the gentle light winds blow,
through the forests of the trees.
It is strongly echoed, loud and clear,
the name ''Shah Rukh Khan'' is the most dear.

MY NAME IS K-K-KHAN

Here's to the universal protagonist,
for as a truly romantic mesmerist,
has captured the principles of dramatism,
with charismatic professionalism.

Bravo to the physical perfectionist,
for as a creational careerist,
has developed diverse art and dramatism,
with chromatic, artistic, estheticism.

Glory to the mega star philanthropist,
for as a rare exclusive idealist,
has promoted his ideals of humanism,
with humble, devoted enthusiasm.

Full marks to our dear eloquent verbalist,
for as a unique conversationalist,
has been exposed to praises of euphemism,
with his humorous, characteristic dynamism.

Kudos to our special educationist,
who developed as a witty linguist,
for producing an hysterical phrenitis
of Mr Kh-Kh-Khan from the epiglottis.

YOU MAKE US LAUGH; YOU MAKE US CRY

You make us laugh; you make us cry.
You make us happy, make us sigh.
In cloudy skies, you are the sun,
Spreading your light to everyone.

On starless nights, you are the moon.
To every song, you are the tune.
You're the lullaby bringing sleep.
The priceless treasure buried deep.

The rainbow in a gloomy sky,
wings of our dreams, you help them fly.
You're the Badshah and our Devdas.
Ruling the present with the past.

On rainy days you make us sing,
like Harry looking for the ring,
You're our Charlie making a plan,
for revenge on a New Year scam.

Charming Raj or lovestruck Sunil.
Bad boy Don and Samar's looks kill.
 Combo of Clooney, Cruise and Pitt,
 as our Rahul you made a hit.

(LAUGH cont'd)

You're Sahir searching for Billu,
or Chef Bablu, cooking the stew.
Dr. Jug, whose lessons we hold.
or Rizwan, with heart of pure gold.

Amazing lover or hero,
 from infinity to Zero,
you don't reflect other stars' light.
Your supernova shines too bright.

Who e're you are, what e're you do;
our hearts know you'll always be true.
All your class, dignity and style,
work together to make us smile!

Endless lists for such a bright star.
You know your stats and who you are.
Your name is praised from East to West.
We fully agree: '' You're the Best''!

ARE YOU FOR REAL?

Tell me sir, "Are you for real"?
I still struggle to believe.
Are you really so pragmatic?
It seems truly enigmatic.

I' m searching for an answer.
It's impossible to find.
Am I suffering delusion?
Is what I see an illusion?

Are you really this perfect?
My logic cannot follow.
My mind thinks it's a deception.
My heart knows you're the exception.

You're so highly accomplished.
Please, explain "how can this be"?
I'm suffering some confusion,
and won't make any allusions.

What is your magic secret?
You must publicly divulge.
You are everybody's vision,
yet I still feel in division.

You are splendidly superb.
You're a world phenomenon!
Thus, I dare to beg you and ask,
''Will you remove your mythic mask''?

(FOR REAL cont'd)

Being such a fantasy,
you're actually fantastic.
Since you excell in each sector,
we are nourished by your nectar.

You are a wild chimera,
though you seem so authentic.
Or perhaps you are a mirage,
appearing as a camouflage?

I shall not burst my bubble.
With my doubts, I won't struggle.
You are my fairy tale charmer,
my brave knight in silver armor.

WHAT IS IT THAT MAKES HIM SO DEAR?

What makes him highly valued?
Before, I couldn't quite tell.
But now I've found the answer,
And know it only too well.

With poets, he's a poet,
An author to those who write.
Suffers with those who suffer,
And speaks up for those who fight.

To patients, he's a doctor.
For parents he's a true son.
In each girl's or woman's dream,
He is the sole number one!

To sisters, he's a brother.
With children, he's a sweet child.
A sacred heart for lovers,
Romantic, tender and mild.

With dreamers, he's a dreamer.
A healer to broken hearts.
To those who have depression,
He helps fix the broken parts.

He surely is an artist,
In all the great fields of Art.
A successful scientist,
When on screen, he plays this part.

(MAKES HIM DEAR cont'd)

With scholars, he's a teacher,
Yet he listens when they speak.
He will guide your emotions
To find the answers you seek.

With dancers, he's a dancer.
A dreamer with those who dream.
A hero in the movies.
A title to every theme.

He's the designers' model.
A fashion icon with grace.
To his fans he's an idol,
Rarely ever loosing face.

One thing's clearly, for certain.
To the world, he is a king.
He's one of us, you and me,
That's why he is ''The real thing''.

OH CAPTAIN, MY CAPTAIN!

Oh Captain, my Captain. I salute you!

So far have you traveled since early days,
walking on sizzling fire, going through dark hell,
my valiant Captain knows only too well.

Battle after battle, you have won wars,
shrugging off old notions and conquering the mind.
You're a brave Captain, true "one of a kind."

Deep in the trenches, you found your way out.
With strategy and patience, victory you gained,
ensuring my Captain, never feels shamed.

The ladder of fame, alone did you climb.
With only your courage and vision as your guide.
The whole army, my Captain, by your side.

(CAPTAIN cont'd)

Neither failure, nor fear made you desert.

Beside the enemy, you refused to conspire.

Therefore, my Captain, it's you we admire!

Fighting with pure guts and claiming your land.

It didn't come easy, you're drenched in sweat and dust,

My determined Captain, you've earned our trust.

Your blind instincts in ambush you followed.

Never did they betray you, but helped save the day.

My Captain's a beacon showing the way.

As an undaunted leader, you were praised.

Your troops were not abandoned, nor did you lose face.

It's my conviction, here I rest my case.

Trophies and medals, sustain your merit

Honor after honor, you glorified your name.

I salute my Captain. You deserve fame!

I HAVE A LIMERENCE ON YOU!

Only for those teary eyes,
that break my heart
and tear it apart,
by shedding a colorful hue.
I have a limerence on you!
Only for those teary eyes!

Only for that dimpled smile,
which spurs romance
and puts us in trance,
spreading warm feelings that ensue.
I have a limerence on you!
Only for that dimpled smile!

Only for that soothing voice.
It's emotion
deepens devotion,
by it's powerful charm to woo.
I have a limerence on you!
Only for that soothing voice!

(LIMERENCE cont'd)

Only for this golden heart,
which strikes a chord
sharper than a sword,
with love that breaks any taboo.
I have a limerence on you!
Only for this golden heart!

Only for those noble traits,
you don with style,
displaying your smile.
What you stand for and boldly do,
making us hope our dreams come true.
I've a limerence on you!

I WISH.....

I wish I could be a tiny drop from the tears you shed,
even the mug holding the steamy coffee you drink.
Maybe the fascinating script for a film you have read,
or the golden pen which has put your words into ink.

What if I were the affectionate glaze in your warm eyes
or the melody of your voice so tender and deep?
I'd like to be the reason for your delightful surprise,
or find the door to enter your sweet dreams when you sleep.

If only I were a stimulating thought on your mind,
which would induce future secret plans to became real.
I wish I could be the comfortable clothes you daily wear,
the soft texture of the delicate fabric you feel.

I would love to be the eloquent speech you keenly wrote,
the wise, inspirational words you carefully choose.
I wish I could be the frame for your most favorite photo,
or perhaps the flash of the camera you always use.

Whatever form I took or wish I had, I do not mind.
If I could exist in your "mythic" world, t'would be fine,
As long as I was a part of your fantastical life.
Only there, in my dreams, you would be forever mine.

STAR LIGHT, STAR BRIGHT

Star light, star bright. I wish I may, I wish I might, have this I wish tonight.

I wish I could meet my star,
who seems so close, but dwells so far.
Like distance from Earth to sky,
you cannot reach, unless you fly.
Therefore, I would wish for wings
to soar up high, as my soul sings.
With birds singing in the air,
songs of joy with the world I'd share.
As Ic'rus flew near the sun.
I'd gaze at my star' til eyes stun,
make me fall on clouds of dreams,
filled with knights, horses, kings and queens.
Like a phoenix burns and dies.
From ashes, I will shine and rise.
Golden wings, wrap fairy light,
to mirror beauty of its sight.
My star's blaze reflects below,
shines by its celestial glow.
Before darkness kisses day,
my wish granted, I'll fly away.
Therefore, my star so light and bright!
Grant me this wish, I wish tonight.

He's the One and Only SRK

He's fa la la, flashy and flame,
He's dashing, dynamic, he's a brand name.
He's sizzling, dazzling, he's hot
With the charming, dishy look he's got.

He's cool, quintessential, he's sway.
He's warmhearted, powerful, he's our bae.
He's got swag, he's a film buff.
He's a superstar and all that stuff.

He's humble and modest, yet still proud.
He can inventively swoon all the crowd.
He's versatile and loyal.
He's inspirational, he's royal.

He's a rock star, he's appealing.
He spreads a ''Shah Rukh Khan'' kinda feeling.
He is persistent and brave.
He's a mythical, flirty, shock-wave.

He's romantic and he's trendy.
He is down to earth and family friendly.
He's grateful, he is giving.
He is generous and forgiving.

(ONE and ONLY cont'd)

He's successful and he's dashing.
He is incandescent and he's smashing.
He's kind and charismatic.
He's artistic and diplomatic.

A mesmerizer, a lover,
As a romancer, he's a real stunner.
He's got talent, he's got style.
He's so cute with his sweet, childish smile.

He's talented, optimistic.
He is keen, polite and idealistic.
He's hardworking, quick witted.
He's enterprising and committed.

A wise man, but a kid at heart.
A natural philosopher who's smart.
He's a winner and self-made.
He's a legend that will never fade.

He's ambitious and breathtaking.
He's communicative and heartbreaking
''Oh Darling''! He's so much fun!
He's the one and only ''Shah Rukh Khan.''!

DEAR ZINDAGI

Dear Zindagi,

    You're full of experience, so your limitless wisdom do impart with whispers of knowledge into our heart.
    Illuminate our dark mind. Our spirit deluge with dedication. Share with us, the fruit of inspiration.
    Reveal the magic secret to develop our body and mind's health. Show us the meaning of inner-wealth.
    Guide us to learn the value of honor and self-appreciation. Enlighten us through deep meditation.
    Take our hands, lead the way, your footsteps to follow, on hopeful paths which will divert our sorrow
    As our mentor, teach us the art of dignity and self-esteem. Heat our passion for fulfilling our dreams.
    Reflect your exuberance. The euphoria will make our soul shine,
with life-lessons and feelings, pure and divine.
    Grant us this aspiration. Engulf our bodies and splendid souls with love and good will to achieve our goals.

THIS ONE'S FOR THE CRYSTAL AWARD

THIS one's for the famous Crystal Award,
    to honor your personal vocation,
    on human rights and social awareness,
    making an exceptional sensation.
THIS one's for the devoted champion,
    with thanks for your inner motivation,
    promoting humanitarian work,
    you were feted for participation.
THIS one's for the celebrated artist.
    For your dedicated contribution,
    improving the state of women victims,
    with your wise, successful resolution.
THIS one is for the glorious privilege
    of achieving historic, worldwide fame.
    Yet again, proving your pragmatic worth
    associated with your father's name.
THIS one's for the incredible journey,
    for taking an unforgettable ride.
    You've taken us to memorable places,
    swelling our hearts with exceptional pride.
THIS one's for the due felicitation
    of a sensitive heart that never sleeps.
    By making your dreams a reality,
    we're made "Yours truly, Forever, For keeps."

ONLY FOR YOU

We know your life isn't only glamour and glitz.
It's mostly scheduled programs and routine.
It's hours of prep to shoot for a scene.

It's fatigue and effort, learning endless lines.
It's restless nights with few hours of calm sleep.
It's tiresome days and thoughts running deep.

It's ups and downs, disappointment and success.
It's traveling to places, always on the go,
Ready to astonish us with the show.

Many hours are spent in gloomy studios,
Enduring physical and inner pain,
In order to superbly entertain.

It's sacrificing hours from family life.
It's missing your kids, as time passes by.
Knowing they'll grow, in the blink of an eye.

It's facing betrayal, yet being gracious
To bitter adversaries and fake foes.
Who seem ready to strike the final blows.

(ONLY FOR YOU cont'd)

It's opening your way with blood, sweat and guts.
Showing merit, without having to stoop.
While your star shines in a secluded group.

It's how you share life lessons with your children,
And other matters which burden your heart.
It's how you choose wisdom you can impart.

We know your life isn't just glitz and glamour.
However, your childhood wish has come true.
We've kept a place in our hearts just ''FOR YOU''.

IS IT REAL OR A UTOPIA?

Then there was the roaring sound of cheering,
and the thunder of clapping and euphemism,
by an ocean of people.
It was the hour of glory at the pinnacle of fame.
When thousands of faces become one burning light,
streaming toward the king's presence.
How can this moment in time be captured?
It must be absorbed in order to saturate,
in every nerve and sinew.
If only the thrill could last forever!
Alas! It's life is limited.
Could it be sealed in a bottle?
Everything is ephemeral and surreal.
The king and his subjects,
so loyal and devoted.
How can they manifest their eternal love?
How can emotions be imparted?
They become a river of sentiments.
Voices cheering with joy.
Feelings stuffed with awe and adoration.
Eyes full of zeal and passion.
Faces beaming with satisfaction.
Everyone desires a piece of their idol.
A touch, a smile, a gesture.
Then the deafening sound of silence.
When lights go out, the soul is empty.
Is it real or an utopia?

"WELCOME PAIN!"

"Welcome" I said. "You are back again."

I know you too well. You are my friend.

In times of sorrow or even bliss,

you come to me with your silent kiss.

With velvet veil, you cover my soul,

and the heavy burden plays its role.

In beloved eyes I seek solace,

until again, I begin the race.

Day or night, you seldom fade away.

You may be hidden but here to stay.

Trying to find me, when I am weak.

You're playing the game of hide and seek.

(WELCOME PAIN cont'd)

Upon my soul you leave your black mark.

When I'm alone, you work in the dark.

I boldly try to find my way out,

but you're deep inside, leaving no doubt.

I know that at the end of the day,

there's just a young boy, fighting his way

to fulfill his dreams with faith and pride,

even at times, sad feelings to hide.

Lights are out and the crowd disappears.

Only then, I let go of my tears.

I've tried to beat you, but all in vain!

Then, it's only I, me, and my pain.

EUPHORIA

It comes as a cascading surge,
with an overwhelming sensation
of goose bumps from head to toe.

A sense of pleasure, excitement,
form a multiple compilation
of feelings which overflow.

When in the full limelight, it breeds,
causing sentiments of revival,
within its presence and style.

In the zeal of my admirers,
I conquer my vital survival,
making me a juvenile!

What a surreal aura it spreads,
while in an ecstasy of sheer glee,
I sense soul and body fly.

I rise above my advocates.
My spirit's on a glorious spree,
my heart rockets to the sky.

It comes, a sudden ardent rush,
my veins are about to wildly burst,
yet, I adhere to a higher tone.

The voice inside me cannot hush,
as I am credibly claimed ''The First'',
I am in the ''twilight zone.''

THE ROAD TO STARDOM

The tough road to stardom
is full of twists and turns.
Mostly crooked, rarely straight,
constantly uphill with many bends,
it's a road that never ends.

A road of solitude,
where many passengers go by.
There'll be endless traffic jams,
and numerous punctures on the way.
It's just another day!

It may seem pure, dazzling.
Sometimes it is, mostly it's not.
With its share of ups and downs,
which make life ordinary and real,
it's not a big deal!

It can be deceptive.
You hardly know who to trust.
Sometimes adored or despised,
always full of hypocrisy and lies.
It's then, you become wise!

It's my road and it's yours.
Regardless of how big or small.
We travel on the same path.
Cause the truth's plain and not so bizarre.
In our world, ''We are the star.''

I WILL HAVE LEFT MY MARK

In each and every step in life,
success became my goal.
I climbed its staggering ladder
with all my heart and soul.

Adventure was my soul journey,
on thorny paths I trod.
I did my part in many jobs,
however plain or odd.

I spared no chance which was given,
my true calling to seek,
and when I found my destiny,
I took it to the peak.

I walked the rough road not taken,
With no one to follow.
I didn't take the easy way,
wrongs I had to swallow.

No patron was there, behind me.
I had to walk alone.
I struggled hard for a good cause.
I made it on my own!

(MARK cont'd)

With effort and dedication.
I played all my cards right.
Ever since I could remember,
I never feared to fight.

For all the people who mattered.
I put on a brave face,
in order to raise up the bar,
hard work did I embrace.

Years later, in my far future,
when days look gray and dark.
I'll look at the trail behind me,
where I'll have left my mark.

TO MY ANGELS IN THE SKY

If you only knew how much I miss you,
especially on a starry night.
I seek to find the two brightest stars,
to warm me with their comforting light.

I stretch my bare, freezing hands to reach you,
to touch the distant, heavenly glow,
while in my lonely heart I feel you,
much closer than you will ever know.

I miss the smiles on your beloved faces,
whenever my troubled soul is blue,
as well as your true words of wisdom
to help me work the typical day through.

My favorite food, I still can remember,
being a comfort to my tiring day,
and your caring love is a lighthouse
to dispel the heavy clouds away.

I miss you at my glorious moments,
when you're loudly absent from my side,
and yearn to hear your gentle voices
to encourage me with special pride.

Your lives have been a shiny guiding light,
that illuminates my unique way,
and whenever I seek your blessing,
I lift my hands to the sky and pray.

2nd of **November**

Heavenly angels sing and good souls pray
humbly for our precious one today.
Tis a day for music, sweet smiles and cheer,
presents and cakes from far and near.
Lots of limitless love, hugs and kisses,
besides dancing, singing and birthday wishes.

On this memorable day, they hold a feast,
from far South to North, and West to East.
With fragrant flowers and buffet dishes,
and festive treats which smell delicious.
For it is such a splendid time of joy,
to all those, who cherish our beloved boy.

Birthday cards are sent wishing all the best,
the family house will welcome his guests.
Events will be held with joy and laughter,
tales of the parties live long after.
Keen fans will honor the celebration,
arranging events with inspiration.

Enthusiastic supporters unite,
to meet and get a glimpse or a sight
of their global icon with devotion,
who stirs our hearts with strong emotions.
He's made his name famous, larger than life
and earned this glory through endless strife.

(2nd of NOVEMBER cont'd)

He will remain ageless and young at heart.
No! Time will never keep us apart!
His movies cover the face of the globe;
with his magic smile, his name he wove.
We can shout it from heaven, down to Earth,
and say "this is the day of our dear son's birth".

Without doubt, the second of November,
will remain a day to remember,
as a tribute to this superstar,
who started from scratch and came so far.
The heavens remain wide open today,
to send our blessing and light his way!

WOMEN OF POWER

Going down the trip on memory lane,
the story in history is always the same.
It is evident behind a great man,
there's a special woman lending her hand.

Therefore, in history, it will remain
that women deserve the real acclaim.
She always works hard behind the curtain.
Her positive results will appear for certain.

She forms past, present, future and beyond
to nurture and create a special bond,
with her father, husband, son, or brother
as one's daughter, wife, sister or mother.

With sacrifice, patience, love and support,
she stands in the shadow without giving report
of pain, exhaustion, agony, sorrow,
or the day's burden after the morrow.

Day in and day out, she's always on guard,
doing her duty, not taking things hard.
She instills values of love and respect,
for her son to embrace and put into effect.

He must understand women are special,
instruments of power, not mere vessels.
In the silence of time, she sheds her light,
teaching her offspring, what's wrong and what's right.

(WOMEN cont'd)

To her spouse she offers words of advice,
as his rock of support in a world full of vice.
Her love is a source of inspirations
to assist him in his obligations.

With dignity, grace she stands by his side,
constantly present she lauds him with pride.
It's no wonder the famous **Shah Rukh Khan,**
is his loving wife's and daughter's most ardent fan.

They have contributed to his success,
something which he never fails to confess.
He acknowledges women do excel,
and gives his thanks for bringing him up well.

Being his prime source of motivation,
he shares his gratitude for the inspiration.
Honoring women with profound respect,
has created a positive effect.

His exceptional brand of love and grace,
always paints a smile on women's face!

TEDTALKS IN INDIA

TedTalks in India? Well, that's a first!
The wisdom of knowledge to millions is dispersed,
creating the realization of a dream,
by witnessing history in the make,
and all this is thanks to Juliet Blake!

However, the heart and soul of the game,
is he who has become synonymous with fame.
And I say this, without intending any pun,
"There's no other person under the sun
as ''priceless'' as India's Shah Rukh Khan!

With fresh innovative ideas and finds
TED's technology, entertainment and designs.
It invites diverse people to speak from the heart
of thoughts which can be an inspiration,
to humans of any generation.

(TEDTALKS cont'd)

It's a revival to bodies and souls,

offering us the best tools to realize our goals

in the game of life, and how to play our own roles.

India should be proud of such a show,

that's viewed by millions, all over the globe.

Praises to the team working behind the scenes,

to the humble host whose personal interest beams.

Shah Rukh Khan's great wit and intelligence, we've seen

played a key role in the show's grand success.

His bright persona is a true ''God bless''!

We're grateful for the visionary mind,

who set up Ted talks to share ideas for mankind,

to embrace challenging perspectives and beliefs.

Thanks to Chris Anderson, new views are spread.

He is the great mastermind behind Ted.

I AM LOVE

No need for words of romance.
No need for a fireworks display,
to show how much I love you
For I am love to stay!

No need for cheerful parties.
No need for champagne flowing free
to make my declaration.
For I am love, you see!

No need for jewels and diamonds.
No need for silver or pure gold
to make a heartfelt statement,
For I am love, ''not sold''.

No need for sweets and presents.
No need for fake red plastic hearts
To offer my affection,
For I am love in Arts.

No need to make a promise,
Or wish on a bright shooting star
to be so close beside you
For I am love, "not far".

No need to echo music,
or wind blowing on your sweet face,
to feel that deep emotion
For I am love, with grace.

No need for church bells ringing
or seeking material wealth
to show my full devotion
For I am love itself!

WHEN I MEET YOU

When I meet you,
The blossoms of trees will shower your presence
with the exquisite colors of nature.
The exotic spices will spread their essence,
to permeate your recognized stature.

When I meet you,
the chiming of bells will greet your arrival,
as an answer to my secret prayer.
The chanting of hymns will lead to revival,
of my soul to hope instead of despair.

When I meet you,
Birds will blend their alluring song,
with the vibes of melody in the air,
as a refreshing breeze, to last all lifelong,
and be gently floating everywhere.

When I meet you,
The skies will open, sprinkling stardust of grace,
with holy blessings, streaming from above.
The sun will shine brighter on your glowing face,
radiating your heart's goodness and love.

When I meet you,
Vivid rainbows will spread their colorful hue,
glittering the path where I'll end my quest
of wishful thinking as in a deja-vu,
when my melting heart begs "Please, be my guest!"

ITHAKA BY C.P. CAVAFY
TRANSLATED BY EDMUND KEELEY

As you set out for Ithaka
hope your road is a long one,
full of adventure, full of discovery.
Laistrygonians, Cyclops,
angry Poseidon—don't be afraid of them:
you'll never find things like that on your way,
as long as you keep your thoughts raised high,
as long as a rare excitement
stirs your spirit and your body.
Laistrygonians, Cyclops,
wild Poseidon—you won't encounter them
unless you bring them along inside your soul,
unless your soul sets them up in front of you.
Hope your road is a long one.
May there be many summer mornings when,
with what pleasure, what joy,
you enter harbors you're seeing for the first time;
may you stop at Phoenician trading stations
to buy fine things,
mother of pearl and coral, amber and ebony,
sensual perfume of every kind—
as many sensual perfumes as you can;

(ITHACA cont'd)

and may you visit many Egyptian cities
to learn and go on learning from their scholars.
Keep Ithaka always in your mind.
Arriving there is what you're destined for.
But don't hurry the journey at all.
Better if it lasts for years,
so you're old by the time you reach the island,
wealthy with all you've gained on the way,
not expecting Ithaka to make you rich.
Ithaka gave you the marvelous journey.
Without her you wouldn't have set out.
She has nothing left to give you now.
And if you find her poor, Ithaka won't have fooled you.
Wise as you will have become, so full of experience,
you'll have understood by then what these Ithakas mean.

A special poem for a special person, written by the famous Greek poet C.P. CAVAFY. He was inspired by the Homeric return journey of Odysseus to his home island ''Ithaka''.

It is not the island but the idea of Ithaca that is important. Life is also a journey therefore…….

THIS IS NOT THE END, ONLY THE BEGINNING.

ABOUT THE AUTHOR

Tania Ioannou is a language teacher who teaches English as a second language to non-native speakers in Greece. She grew up in Australia as a child of Greek-Australian immigrants.

She has written poetry in Greek which has been published in local magazines. For the love of Shah Rukh Khan, Tania has written this collection of 27 poems for his 27 years in Showbiz.

This work was an outlet for the grief she suffered after the loss of her 23 year-old daughter in a car accident. Tania is a supporter of humanitarian work and believes in kindness and gratitude.

Tania welcomes feedback on her work and always loves to hear from her readers. You can reach her at the following email address:

thomaio6@hotmail.gr

She is also active on Twitter: @tania_ioannou

Printed in Great Britain
by Amazon